CW00429053

Hidden Beauty

Facets of the Good News from the Garden

by
Joan Foster
Illustrated by
Andrea Grealy

MOORLEY'S Print & Publishing

© Copyright 2000

All rights reserved. No part of this publication may be
reproduced, stored in a retrieval system, or
transmitted, in any form or by any means,
electronic, mechanical, photocopying, recording
or otherwise, without the prior
written permission of the publishers.

British Library Cataloguing in Publication Data.
A catalogue record for this book is available
from the British Library.

ISBN 0 86071 540 X

MOORLEY'S Print & Publishing
23 Park Rd., Ilkeston, Derbys DE7 5DA
Tel/Fax: (0115) 932 0643

Contents

Ᏺidden Beauty

Ᏺt was the middle of October and the misty, damp weather was just right for picking out the numerous spiders' webs that were around.

The cobwebs were everywhere. Evergreen trees were covered by webs of every size. They were across the windows. On one window, four strands stretched to the four corners and a fascinating and intricate web filled the centre of the pane. A beautifully-marked spider sat in the middle. When the lady went out of the door, she was met by the sight of a city of cobwebs... across the door, the shed, the tubs and all over the lawn. She was loathe to open the wheelie-bin lid because a web had been carefully spun from there to a garden chair. What a sight! Cobwebs everywhere... dripping with moisture... and they only showed up because of the damp.

Here was a world of hidden beauty... breathtaking and indescribable. As the sun came out and the moisture dried up, many of the cobwebs disappeared from immediate sight... It was very difficult to see them, although they were still there. The lady had to look hard and, had she not already known of their existence, she would have missed them. She thought of all that hidden beauty... all the wonder of those cobwebs that had transformed the garden and lifted her heart...

She thought of hidden beauty in general...

There is so much hidden beauty inside each one of us... so much hidden beauty in the lives of people around us. There is so much inside that can be beautiful. We are all made by God, with personalities, gifts, thoughts and feelings. So much lies inside every person, waiting to be picked out and shown up, just like those cobwebs. There is the latent ability to love, to care, to give, to respond, to be... Dormant gifts and attitudes are all there... waiting for the touch of God to illuminate them... to bring them out into the open... to make them stand out.

When God does touch them, we become beautiful people... beautiful in Him... showing His glory and beauty to the world. Our actions reflect our God. Our words are His words. Our attitudes become like His. What a wonderful thought... that He takes what He has already given... that he touches what He has already placed inside us... and makes it like Him, transformed into His likeness. The hidden beauty is revealed for all to see... a gift from God originally... so graciously given back to us and to all who see us.

There is more hidden beauty. So much love and care goes on between people, unknown to anyone but the people concerned and God. We know about the support that is asked for, about the help that is given for a seen problem or request... but so many beautiful acts of kindness and consideration take place in response to a need suddenly noticed, a silent cry for help. Some people have that beautiful gift... the gift of recognising and responding to a silent cry... the gift of understanding what is needed even before the need is acknowledged or put into words... of pre-empting the situation and offering the word or look of help or encouragement just as it is needed.

This is the hidden beauty which we rarely see. The daily acts of kindness, of support, which go unnoticed... the phone calls, the words, written and spoken, the little gifts, the smile, the glance... all of which can make such a difference to someone... all of which are seen only as a reflection, as it were... in the uplifting of someone who was low, in the renewing of the determination of someone who was faltering or in the positive action of someone who was confused by negative thoughts. We see hidden beauty in the support of one person for another... in the acts of gentleness and concern... in courage against difficulties or illness and injury.

The appearance of some young people nowadays does not always fit in with what we necessarily expect or "approve"... whether or not we have the right to make that judgement. Yet they are often well spoken, polite and friendly. It can be good to talk with them... Hidden beauty... and it is there in so very many of our young people today... as they tend to look what they are not... to behave as they are not... to cry out to be recognised, accepted and loved for what they are... deep down inside... where so often they hurt and feel lost.

There is a place inside us that is God... whether we know Him personally or not. It is there to be seen in everyone, yet it shows so much more when it is touched by God Himself... when we acknowledge His Presence in our lives... when we allow Him to shine out through us. Then, our hidden beauty is no longer hidden... It is there, clear and obvious... open... for all to see... and all who see must surely recognise our God in us... and hopefully want what we have... the radiant beauty of God-with-us... Immanuel.

Mutual Support

Every so often, we need re-fuelling. Life holds its concerns... which come to a climax from time to time... and emotionally and mentally we need re-fuelling. At such times, friends are quickly there for us. They pray with us and help God to begin to restore some equilibrium and peace into us.

When we weep, they weep for us... feeling our pain... sharing our hurt. They feel our fragility, share our anguish... hurt inside with us. It Is a moving thought... to be so loved and supported... to know the care of precious friends.

The gardener looked across his garden and looked with fresh eyes at the border near the ash tree. It was such a mixture of plants... a variety, really, of what could actually manage to grow there, for the tree's roots took up so much room and drank the water when it rained.

7

The rambling rose looked beautiful... covered in pink buds which were just beginning to open. A honeysuckle was twined amongst it. It had been stood there a couple of years ago whilst the gardener decided where to put it and never actually dug into the ground! The red, papery-looking poppies were huge and hardly seemed real. There were cornflowers, tiger lilies and lupins and then a group of ivy, periwinkle, cotoneaster and potentilla... all inter-twined... a haphazard display.

Further along, there was some yarrow, given to him by a friend some years ago. A rose called "Silver Wedding" was in bud. That was bought two years ago by his neighbours as he and his wife celebrated their anniversary. Next to it was "Peace"... a rose which some visitors had bought for them.

In the space of a few metres there was such a variety of life... of age... of appearance... growing together... and many of the plants were, literally, supporting one another. None were apart... none looked out of place... and all made their contribution to the overall effect... That's like people within their Church Fellowships...

Many of the plants were inter-twined... they were actually <u>depending</u> upon one another for support. They were not fastened to the fence... The shoots of one were threaded through those of another, so that, for example, the newly-established honeysuckle was depending upon the firmly-rooted rambling rose and parts of the ivy trailed through the cotoneaster. In another border, there was a beautiful show of honeysuckle, which was actually growing up a holly tree and covering that dark bush with colour.

The plants were supporting one another and were inter-dependent... Just like us. There are times when we hurt... and in our fellowships we share that hurt. It is wonderful that we can immediately share our pain... a phone call, a visit, a shared word... and we are immediately relieved of some of the pain that would otherwise go deeper and hurt more.

There's no need for explanation... no having to try to describe feelings. We see one another's faces... hear our voices... and we <u>know</u>. It doesn't matter initially what has happened. There is prayer and love, support and acceptance... and someone to <u>hear</u>. The hurt begins to lift, the tears gradually stop and prayer soothes the inner turmoil. God is with us. He draws nearer to us all and we draw nearer to one another. We may well feel fragile for a while. The emotions may be delicate and there may be things to sort... but the initial impact has been lightened.

That border also held many memories. Of course, we are not meant to live in the past... but memories form our present and our future. They mould us. They provide the experiences on which we build and whether happy or sad, they become precious to us. The potentillas were birthday presents and reminded the gardener of a friend who had since moved away. There was 'Yarrow', 'Silver Wedding' and 'Peace'. Then there was the rambling rose, a cutting from his father-in-law's garden taken just before he died.

We, too, share memories. Although we are looking ahead... sharing a vision for our Church and plans for our lives... nevertheless the depth of our friendship is built on shared memories... of Fellowship and special times of worship together... of precious moments exchanged... of the joy of celebrating together... birthdays, wedding anniversaries... of tears when a loved one dies... of anxiety over physical pain... of hurt feelings... of disappointment or uncertainty...

"There is a time for everything,
and a season for every activity under heaven:
a time to be born and a time to die,
a time to plant and a time to uproot....
a time to weep and a time to laugh,
a time to mourn and a time to dance...."
Ecclesiastes 3:1, 2, 4

There is a time for every human feeling...
-    and we have shared them...
-    and so the love grows deeper... the support stronger.
Let us at all times thank God for the strength and availability of that support.

There's Always Something New

The teacher had a lot of work to do and, at first, he was not being very self-disciplined. It was a wet and windy Saturday afternoon and he had sat still for a while! He wanted to see what was happening in the garden. He wanted to walk out in the wind and collect the conkers which he knew were bound to be flying through the air and landing all over the place. They would be useful for a lesson next week.

He wandered into the kitchen to eat some grapes from the dish. They were sweet and juicy, so he drifted past a few times to collect some more and then he happened to be near the 'phone, so he rang his friend. The friend was kind and understanding, as always, making allowances for the teacher's lack of self-discipline... finding logical reasons for his not settling down and saying "there is always something new to find." He had recently found more buds on a miniature rose bush in his garden and clematis flowers opening in the middle of October.

There is always something new to find! That's why the teacher found it hard to settle. Why he wanted to be outside. He'd found a new cyclamen flower on his little Autumn-flowering cyclamen plants and he wanted to see if any more were uncurling their heads.

The squirrel had been digging in one of the tubs and sent the pansies flying and he wanted to re-plant them for the 'tenth' time. The apples on his daughter's tree were turning red and he wanted to take their photograph before they fell off. There were a hundred and one things to seek out. He was restless with the excitement of adventure on that windy afternoon and he felt a sense of anticipation...

There's always something new to find out about our God, always new depths to explore in our relationship with Him, always something new to discover in His word.

Do we feel the same delight in finding out fresh things about our God as the teacher felt when he found a new flower...?

God never ceases to amaze. We see Him at work every day, in our lives and in the lives of others. Do we retain the freshness of amazement at His works or do we simply take it all for granted, or hardly even notice? "Every day dawns beautiful with promise", and the teacher wondered if we meet it with the excitement that that signifies.

10

There is always something new even in the way the light shines through at the beginning of the day, depending on the clouds and the clarity of the sky. There is always something new in the appearance of the trees and flowers, as the leaves change colour or open on the trees and as the flowers grow, open and fade. There is always something new as the birds come into the garden and dig for worms or eat the berries. There's always something new to watch.

We meet people and see something new in them each day. We have all prepared for the day with particular feelings, so when we come together, we meet on a new level every time. There are so many possible combinations of where we are all at, so we see one another afresh every time we meet. There is a joy to be found every time we are with people, seeing what is new in them.

There is always something new to be found in a flower... in a tree... in a dear person's face... in a growing relationship... in the reaction of an animal. There is always something new to be found in the growth and response of a new life... in the shape of the clouds... in the play of light and shadow across land or water... in the development of a child...

There is always something new to be found in God and there lies the greatest wonder of all. His Living Word is forever new. No matter how well we think we know it, no matter how familiar the well-loved words, they still reveal a freshness, a new, deeper meaning whenever we study them. They grow with us as we mature as Christians, revealing more and more about our God... showing new aspects of His character and a deeper insight into Him. More study of God's Living Word also reveals new meaning in its teaching, so we learn constantly from it. It is always fresh, always new... the Living Word which feeds a Living Church...

...And so, shouldn't there be room for new things within the Church, too? Shouldn't there be change, and growth? If "the Church", the Body of Christ, is made up of individuals, living people who are constantly changing and being made new in Christ, shouldn't the Church itself be for ever changing and growing? Jesus said, "Behold, I make all things new." When we know and love Him as our Lord, we become a new creation, and from that moment on, we continue to be made new in Him.

So the Church can hardly remain static. We cannot possibly ignore thoughts of new music, phraseology or methods of worship. That is not to say that we abandon the old. We are the same basic people before and after we know Jesus personally. He simply builds on what we are, touching us with His Holy Spirit, so that we gradually become new in Him. We do not suddenly become physically unrecognisable. In the same way we keep our basic Faith, our foundation within our Church, but we build on it, changing and adapting as the years go by, moving with the changing times, yet remaining faithful to the commands of God... not becoming suddenly unrecognisable. We are greatly blessed by the newness of everything – not sudden, threatening change, but a freshness; a new delight each day as everything remains similar yet is ever-changing.

So let us rejoice in our God, who provides such beauty, such joy and excitement and who brings something new into our lives every day, whilst remaining our Rock, our foundation, our changeless, yet ever-changing God.

There is always one...

$\mathcal{A}$s the man left Church, he looked again at the daffodil which he had noticed a few days before near the Church gates.

There was actually a clump of daffodils, all pointing towards the sun, all, that is, except for one. A single daffodil was pointing in totally the opposite direction and it looked so conspicuous.

The man studied it again. It was tall and straight, just like the others. It was beautiful... fully open... but it had its back to the sun and he pondered over this. A large group of daffodils... and just one so pointedly facing in the opposite direction... It was not just the opposite direction but the direction which seemed unnatural... the one which did not give the best light and warmth to the flower head.

Of course the daffodil had not chosen to face that way. It was the way it was growing... something which the man could not understand, a fluke of nature, as it were... but it did make him think of people. God is our source of light and life and we are advised to turn towards Him in order to grow and flourish to our true potential. Yet some people turn their backs.

It is a deliberate move. We are given free choice. God created us to love Him, but love cannot be forced. It has to grow out of free will and so God runs the risk of being rejected, of people turning their backs on Him. He does all that He can to encourage us to love Him. Throughout the

Bible, God advises us to choose life, that is, to turn to Him. There are several references to this, including the actual command in Deuteronomy, Chapter 30.

"See, I set before you today life and prosperity, death and destruction. For I command you today to love the Lord your God, to walk in His ways, and to keep His commands... But if your heart turns away and you are not obedient... you will certainly be destroyed... This day I call heaven and earth as witnesses against you that I have set before you life and death, blessings and curses. Now choose life, so that you and your children may live."

Throughout the Old Testament, we see God's longing for us to turn towards Him. He yearns for us to receive His love, His life... and in the New Testament, we see how God even sent His own dearly loved Son into the world to die for us and to show us the way to God. In John, chapter 14 verse 6 we read,

"Jesus answered, 'I am the way the truth and the life. No-one comes to the Father except through me.'"

We know the blessings which God gives when people do turn to face Him. We know the joy, the peace, the love. We know that a life given to God is not a life lost but a life gained:

"For whoever wants to save his life will lose it, but whoever loses his life for me and for the gospel will save it." Mark 8:35

Yet some people still turn their backs, either deliberately or because they do not know of the life which God offers. What can we do for them? When we know of all that God has to give, we so want others to share the blessings. We can show them the fruits of a life given to God. We can show them patience and tolerance. We can show them understanding when they least expect it... and we can show them love. Through God's grace, we can love them ...and love can overcome all things. Love can conquer hatred and uncertainty, fear and suspicion... and love alone can point to God... the complete love of Jesus, who gave His life in a sacrificial act of love... Our love, imperfect and hesitant though it may be, nevertheless, is from God... for God is love.

We can love those people who have turned their backs on God... and we can pray for them. Let us never underestimate the power of prayer.

In all of St. Paul's letters, he urges the early Christians to pray for one another. Jesus Himself not only taught us how to pray, but by His frequent example, He showed us the importance of constant prayer. Jesus Himself is our Intercessor, as we lift one another and all people, whichever way they may be facing, up to Almighty God.

As we pray for others, let us never forget to pray, in all humility, for one another and for ourselves. There are times when <u>our</u> eyes are not always facing the right direction... times when we may be tempted to face the wrong way... times when it may seem easier for the moment, to look away from God.

May we pray for the strength and the desire always to face fully in the direction of our God and to draw on His light and love. May we pray for an urgent longing to want to turn other people in that same direction, so that we may be blessed together.

A New Creation

$\mathbf{T}$he elderly man was enjoying his garden early one morning. It was glorious. A crisp early Spring morning showed the promise of a joyous day to come.

Everything was fresh. Although the sky was blue, it was that special blackbird-egg-colour-blue of early Spring, rather than the deep azure blue of Summer. The green of next door's willow tree was almost a lime green in its brightness and there was the yellow... everywhere, the yellow... forsythia, primulas and daffodils.

The daffodils took his breath away.. daffodils of every shape and size, from the tiny tete-a-tete species to the tall, majestic King Alfred with their large golden trumpets. They were in various stages of opening, just like us... and they looked so beautiful.

As the man studied the perfection of those daffodils, he thought of how we are all gradually opening – opening up to God and to one another. He thought of how God so wants us to be fully open, to reveal our full and true beauty.

We close in sometimes, a bit afraid to show our full selves... for that reveals our vulnerability and the parts of us of which we perhaps feel ashamed. God is not ashamed of us. He knows that we get things wrong at times. He knows that we can be irritable and impatient, intolerant or unreasonable. He sees our vulnerability and our "weaknesses." He's the one who created us... Yet He never stops loving us. Indeed, it is when we are fragile that He loves us more. It is when we show the parts of us which we feel are not so nice to know and then come to God in genuine sorrow, that He cares even more for us. He embraces us, picks us up and sets us on our feet for another try... just as a human father does for his young child. He loves us through every thought and deed.

It is a sign of true Christian love that we can come together in complete openness... and still feel loved and loveable, still be accepted, still feel a joy in one another. As we see one another's "weaknesses"... the tears, the frustrations, the hurt feelings, the anger... so our Christ-like love deepens... So we grow more protective towards one another, more supportive as we all make our way along our journey of faith.

The beauty of the Spring garden was even more special because it was in such a stark contrast to what it had been like during the winter. Although, as God's creation, the garden is always lovely... just as we are... the winter garden does tend to lack colour and joy. It can look rather bleak. The Spring garden has a joy about it. It has a freshness and brightness... a touch of hope and expectation as it foretells the promise of the vibrancy of Summer... and so it is for us.

We are always beautiful... in God's eyes and in one another's... even if we don't always feel it. Yet how glorious we are when we emerge from a bleak or barren spell... when we open up afresh after a time of pain or desolation... when we tentatively unfurl and feel again the warmth, love and care of our God and of our friends.

We may not feel it, but we are at our best after a difficult time. We carry new growth in Christ, new beauty, new radiance, new life. We have a new hope and a new joy. We are a new creation in Him!

In 2 Corinthians, chapter 5 verse 17, Paul writes,

"Therefore, if anyone is in Christ, he is a new creation; the old has gone, the new has come!"

... and in the Book of Revelation, we are given that wonderful assurance,

"He who was seated on the throne, said,

'I am making everything new!'" Revelation 21:5

In The Right Place

The middle-aged woman loved her garden and she had been working hard in it. She was mainly putting in bedding plants... arranging them in tubs and borders.

The actual planting didn't take long. It was the thinking about which plants were suitable for where... which would look best together because of colour and habit... which would be best in certain parts of the borders because of height and the need for sun or for protection from the wind... which would be best near the house because of fragrance and effect. It all took a lot of thought. It was important. It made such a difference to the final effect and to the colourful beauty of the garden during the summer months. It was important that the plants were in the right place so that they could give the best impression and be most effective.

It's the same with us. How important it is that we are in the right place... filling the right space so that our God-given gifts can be used to the best effect... so that we can be used and seen at our best for God. It's no use trying to force someone to undertake tasks for which they are unsuitable or ill-equipped. Yes, if a task is right for someone, God provides the wherewithal to see it through, but in such cases, God Himself causes the person to "feel" that it is right. He prods and nudges until whoever it is becomes aware that they should be fulfilling a particular requirement. That is very different from someone being placed in a position, which simply isn't right.

It is not good for someone who is reserved and slow to speak to new people, to take on the task of welcoming people to the services or of serving refreshments at Church functions, for example. People doing that job need to be relaxed with themselves, so that others relax on arrival and feel comfortable with where they are. They need to be able to show an interest in others and make them feel important. It is a gift, which not everyone has and it is a mistake for the wrong people to try to do the job, for it greatly affects people's impressions. What a vital task... and the wrong people doing it are preventing others from using their very special ministry.

It's the same with everything. Whatever our ministry, we are called to use it to the glory of God and for the furtherance of His Kingdom. If we try to do other things for which we are not equipped, we are erring in two ways. One, <u>we</u> are not filling that place correctly and two, we are preventing those who should fill it from doing so.

There is a place for everyone. We are all abundantly blessed by God... not only because He loves us but also because He needs us to do His work here on earth. He wants us to show His love to the world and to bring others into a close relationship with Him. We are equipped differently in order to undertake the various aspects of His work. No-one is left out. It is up to us, with God's guidance, to discover our strengths and weaknesses, to find our 'right' place and so to use our full potential for Him. This is where general support and prayer are so vital. We need to pray for, help and advise one another. Others can often see more clearly where someone else's ministry lies. Others can be used as sounding boards for a person feeling God's 'push' in a certain direction and wanting to verify those feelings. We need to be open and honest with one another, both in question and in response, about the appropriateness of a particular task for us. We need not be afraid of a certain area being wrong... another will be very right.

Although we think of the 'right place' for us in God's order of things, that does not mean that we find our ministry and then that 'is it'. We are not static for life. Our gifts develop and grow. Our ministries change. Over the years, because of our human circumstances... which God ordains... we are called to do different works for Him. That is why it is so essential that we remain open to Him... that we listen to His voice... that we share with others, advising and supporting one another. We need constantly to be listening to God's instructions and weighing what we hear with the guidance, which God is giving, within our Fellowship.

The young mother with a toddler may find that it suits their routine very well to be on the Church cleaning rota and to go together to dust and polish. Once the child is at school, that young mother may find herself with a little more available time to visit the elderly or sick, something which she could not do with a young child. God could well indicate that she has a gift for that kind of work within the parish. She is wise to listen. Not all are called to such visiting. She can fulfil a vital role in the community and carry God's love into the homes of others... and someone else with a toddler may well be seeking her right place for God. For the first mother to hold on to the cleaning could be depriving someone else of a ministry as well as failing to undertake what God has in store for her next.

Our ministries change, too, with older age. In our later years, we may well become less physically active and not able to take on some of the tasks involved in the Church. We may not be able to maintain the Churchyard or decoration of the Church, but we can make a cup of tea for those who are able. We may not be able to walk round the Parish on a prayer walk, but we can sit at home and pray for those who are. The precious ministry of prayer must never be underestimated. It is the foundation on which our Church grows.

So we are never out of a job! Every gift, every ministry, is of equal value. No one is more important than the other. The vital thing is that we all find our right ministry for that particular time... always open and alert to God's changing instructions as we change and develop and as our circumstances alter.

We know when we are 'in the right place'. We feel God's peace... Others see Him in us... and God's Kingdom grows.

Preparation

It was a glorious morning... bright and sunny but with a cold wind which made it fresh and exhilarating for walking.

As the couple walked along the lane towards the fields they were amazed to see one or two snowdrops in full flower. They were just glorying in this fact, when they saw several clusters in the grass verge. They stooped to look at the simple beauty of the flowers. It was such a surprise and pure pleasure to see them, for theirs were not that far advanced. They realised that these open flowers were in the full sun, whereas theirs were sheltered by shrubs.

The sight of those snowdrops reminded the couple of the verse:

"Nothing is so strong as gentleness, nothing so gentle as real strength."

Snowdrops look fragile. Their leaves are slender, their stems thin and the flowers themselves are so delicate. Yet they are amongst the first of the flowers to appear at the beginning of the year, whilst it is still Winter. Snowdrops begin to appear whilst the ground is still hard with frost and often covered with snow. They grow during the worst of our cold, wet winter weather.

As the couple studied the green-edged, frilled flowers, they shared thoughts of how the flower had been coming up through the ground, growing and even opening, before people ever dared to begin to think of looking for them. The days can be dark, cold, wet... we carry on with our tasks... concentrating on completing our daily business, sometimes feeling that it's a bit of a haul through the worst of the winter... never thinking to look for things like snowdrops! By the time we think about it, they are already well through and showing at least the promise of their white flowers even if they are not actually open... All of this has been happening quietly, unnoticed and often through the worst of conditions... and so it is that these gentle flowers illustrate hidden strength.

We meet some people like that... gentle in spirit, seemingly fairly quiet, humble... and yet who possess an inner strength which is so obvious in times of difficulties both for themselves and for other people. They possess an inner quality which exudes gentle strength, reliability, calmness and wisdom... and from which others gain confidence and support.

We see nature preparing all the time for what is yet to come... under cover, underground, on the quiet... Roots spread and take in goodness, bulbs fill out and send up shoots, leaf and flower buds form... growth takes place largely unnoticed until, one day, we are suddenly aware that something has grown, blossomed, produced flowers, leaves or fruits...

God seems to work like that. He knows what lies ahead in our lives. He knows what preparation we need in order to be ready for what is coming next. He knows if we are ready or if a few alterations are necessary. God often uses the times when we are experiencing difficulties to prepare us for a future task which He will require us to undertake. We may have difficulty with a relationship at work, only to find that the practice of dealing with that situation is to stand us in good stead for dealing with other people whom we come across both inside and outside our Church Fellowship.

We may find ourselves working though a former inner hurt, which seems to have arisen inexplicably... only to discover that that pain needed to be sorted and removed before we were free to cope with a task for God. We may find ourselves struggling with something within our personality which God insists that we overcome so that we can work more effectively for Him.

At the time of these difficulties, we have no idea of what God has in mind. We only know that something is happening, that some change is

taking place, some problem being worked through. It can be difficult...
but it is all in God's hands. We come through stronger and better
equipped for Him.

We do begin to recognise these signs. It is possible for us to begin to
know that God is preparing us for something ahead. We can sometimes
see that He is strengthening us in what has been a weaker area,
equipping us with gifts that were never previously developed in us,
causing a vulnerable area inside to surface and be healed.

It can be painful and tiring... but what a privilege! How wonderful to
think that we are <u>that</u> important to God. We are each such a small being
in His vast creation... yet we matter <u>that</u> much. Each one of us is so
important to God that He wants to use us for His work. He is prepared to
use infinite patience so that we are ready to do His work... and He wants
us to grow personally as well.

What a privilege to be His children!

"Let him Easter in us,
be a day-spring to the dimness of us."

Gerard Manley Hopkins.
'The Wreck of the Deutschland'

A New Confidence

It was time for putting the bedding plants into the garden. As the young woman dug the holes for her plants she felt that she was "doing her bit" towards feeding the present generation of baby birds.

A starling and robin had been hovering around where she had been digging, but she actually began to make friends with a blackbird. He gradually became very tame. As she dug the holes, the blackbird was almost putting his beak into them! He was no doubt grateful for having his job made easier as he filled his beak with grubs and worms, going about the endless task of feeding his young family.

The blackbird flew down almost as soon as the woman began to garden and he came so close that she wanted to reach out and stroke him. His black and orange eyes were bright, but his feathers looked a bit dull and straggly. He was probably too exhausted after hurrying around feeding his babies all day to want to preen himself before going to bed. He was looking rather thin.

The young woman was amazed at his daring. She had never seen a blackbird so close. She thought of courage and of how this bird was driven to an unusual and greater confidence by the inner need to feed his young family. He was driven on by something greater and more powerful than himself... something which overcame his natural instincts of caution and fear.

She thought of people whom she knew who had recently spoken of a new confidence... a new confidence in God, which came over as being more assured in themselves.

So often, we hesitate humanly over so many things. We can feel the need to speak to someone about a matter and hesitate in case we do not have the right words. It may be someone recently bereaved. It may be that someone is not doing things in the right way and some form of correction is necessary. It may be that a suggestion is necessary for guidance. We can hesitate for so many reasons.... yet feel the weight inside pushing us on to speak. We can feel drawn to do something new... leading the prayers, reading the lessons, working with the children in church, becoming involved with something at work. Again, we can hesitate as we doubt our ability.

We can lack confidence in ourselves... we can have our confidence sapped so easily by others... but God does not want us to be like that. He wants us to walk with our heads high. That thought immediately raises the question of a balance between being confident as children of God and yet humble as God's servants. We are not speaking of the pushing confidence which is not acceptable... nor are we supposed "to boast". Arrogance puts one person above another and that is not spiritual... but, so often, British people do not speak of their gifts or achievements for fear of being accused of "showing off". We are a fairly reticent and withdrawn race in so many ways.

When someone has done well, we should feel free to give credit and praise where it is due. Why not, with justifiable pride, be able to acknowledge a child's hard work and achievements? Why are we not encouraged to say, "Yes, I can do that"... "I'm good at that"... "That is my gift". There are few things more beautiful to the ears than such a phrase... said in humility and confidence... for our ability comes from God and should be acknowledged.

Our new confidence in ourselves grows as we develop a new confidence in God. Day by day, as we walk with Him, we discover more and more that He is totally trustworthy. The realisation that He will not let us down becomes deeper. In little things and in big, He will always sustain us and provide what is necessary. When we have to speak with someone, He will give the right words. If what we are doing is right, God will also provide the situation and prepare the heart of the person involved to receive what has to be said... and it will be said in love... His love. God will bless such times, supervising them personally... and our confidence will grow... confidence in ourselves and in Him, for He equips us for every task which He sets before us.

We may hesitate about what we feel called to do... shrinking back because "I couldn't possibly..." Yet if it is right, God will give us the ability to do it... as we are driven on by a power inside that is greater than us... the power of God... the power of the Holy Spirit... given to us to go out into the world and preach the Good News... given to us to empower us... given to us so that we might have confidence... not in ourselves necessarily, but in our God... who enables us to do all things for Him... who never lets us down... who always provides... and always equips us.

We walk in humility as God's servants... but in confidence as His loved children.

ℏe Is Not ℏere; ℏe ℏas Risen
(Luke 24:6)

The gardener was pottering in the greenhouse amongst the seedlings. It was a wonderful relief to look again at the vine and see the healthy new buds opening daily into fresh, green leaves.

Not long ago, he thought he had killed the vine. The frost had come early that winter and he had left some of his Autumn gardening. Earlier in the year he had gone back into the greenhouse. The weather had been cold and the greenhouse had been a mess, left with things lying around. The dark branches of the vine had been growing over half of the glass. Some dead leaves had still clung to the vine whilst others had been lying on the soil. It had felt cold and dark in there...

The gardener had taken the secateurs and cut away at the branches in an effort to clear the greenhouse and let in some light. He had been rather ruthless with his pruning... especially at a time of such heavy frosts. He had thought no more of it and had not gone into the greenhouse again for quite a while.

As the weather warmed up, he returned to the greenhouse to prepare for sowing his seeds. The vine looked bare... not a sign of a bud. Perhaps it was too early? Perhaps he had killed it? For the first time, he thought that his vicious pruning may indeed have been unwise. He had always cut the vine well back... but did he usually do it that much? and in the depth of winter? For the first time, anxiety crept in... But there was nothing he could do about it then.

27

He began to make regular trips to the greenhouse in order to peer at the buds. Was it his imagination, or were they filling out? It was his imagination. However, one day, he <u>could</u> see a change in the shape of the buds. They <u>were</u> fatter. Since then, they had filled out daily in the warmth of the sun and the healthy green leaves were beginning to show.

"It takes more than that to destroy an established vine. You can't kill it off that easily... No, you can't... Nor can you kill God." It was hard to put his fleeting, almost subconscious thoughts into words... but they were something like that.   Having the Biblical picture of the vine constantly in his mind whenever he went into the greenhouse, he could not help but liken what had happened to his vine with what we did to our God.

He had treated the vine harshly and rather cruelly, he realised... more or less without thinking of the situation, conditions and possible consequences. It was similar, in a more mild way, to the way in which the world treated Jesus when He was put to death. It was similar to the way in which we treat Him every time we sin. We continue to press the crown of thorns on His head, to reject Him, mock Him, hammer in the nails... to crucify Him.

We so often don't think.... Whatever we do to others, we do to Jesus. When we are thoughtless or insensitive and so hurt people, we hurt Jesus. When we are selfish or unkind, we drive another nail into Jesus. When our thoughts are only for ourselves and we feel that we have no time to give to others, we crucify our Lord. We don't mean to do it. The gardener had not meant to jeopardise the chances of his vine's survival.

We don't always think. Many people did not think 2,000 years ago when they had Jesus put to death. In many ways, it was an unfortunate series of events... but it was pre-ordained by God, because He was not going to be defeated by death. You can't kill God. All those years ago, He conquered death and rose again, glorious and victorious from the tomb. This time of seeming tragedy was, in fact, God at His most triumphant... overcoming the greatest evil that we can ever begin to imagine. Not only did God triumph – He turned that darkest moment into a time of positive action and growth... building a new people... His Church.

So now, to our shame, we crucify Jesus time after time. Yet He is not defeated. He refuses to die. Over and over again He pours His blessings upon us. He forgives us, lifts us, strengthens us. He equips us to do better. He smiles at our sometimes feeble efforts. He turns our failures into successes, our weakness into strength, our darkest moments into times of light, triumph and growth. Why?...

... Because He loves us... because we are His children... because He wants everyone to know Him and receive the benefits which life with Him brings... because He wants to show us that our darkest moments, too, can become positive and triumphant.

For the children of God, there are no rights, simply numerous privileges... and those are what He wants to pour upon us. That is why He is prepared to suffer daily. He is building a people of power... and, even in our inadequacy, we are instrumental in helping Him.

Praise Him. Lord, have mercy.
"Greater love has no-one than this, that he lay down his life for his friends." John 15:13

"For I'm building a people of power,
and I'm making a people of praise,
that will move through this land by my Spirit,
and will glorify my precious name.

Build your church, Lord,
Make us strong Lord,
join our hearts, Lord, through your Son;
Make us one, Lord, in your body,
In the kingdom of your Son."
Mission Praise 151

"He turns our weaknesses into His opportunities..."

New Life – 1

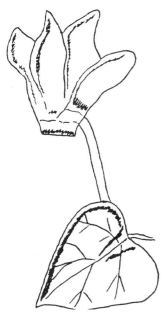

If questioned about it, we would perhaps say that Autumn is basically a time when plants die down in preparation for their winter rest and new growth in the Spring. We don't think too much about new life in the Autumn.

The garden was suddenly looking particularly autumnal, with much of the summer colour only a memory. The lady went outside to rake up some leaves and to plant some bulbs, and was overjoyed when she discovered beautiful new growth in her garden.

She had spent ages the previous year looking for her Autumn flowering cyclamen on the grassy slope where she had so carefully planted them. She had been disappointed when nothing had appeared and she had given them up as lost. She had not given them a thought or a glance since, but there they were... two tiny clumps of perfect flowers with more buds pushing up through the lawn.

The lady crouched down and looked in amazement at the perfect beauty of each flower, but, more than that at the fragility of those fleshy, bent stems. The ground was rock-hard, part sheltered under a shrub and very dry. She could not imagine how something so frail had managed to push its way up through that soil. Not only had it pierced the surface of the ground, it had also produced something of real beauty when everything else was dying down.

Each flower stood out. Each was tiny... fragile-looking but obviously not fragile at all. It was making its own, very special contribution to the Autumn garden.

The lady thought of people. She thought of when we feel particularly fragile for various reasons... and we do sometimes... through illness, bereavement, past hurts, tiredness. She thought of the verse in 2 Corinthians about God being strong when we are weak... and she thought of the special contribution which we can still make in this world for God, even when we feel incapable, tired, to fragile. God takes over and, provided we are prepared to be used, He does all the hard work.

We just have to grow.

Middle-aged herself, she thought of when we are in the autumn of our lives. It was rather lovely to think that God can use us in the autumn of our lives... There's no dying-off and sitting back for us. God can use us afresh and in a wonderful way... to stand out in the world in His strength. Our ministry is never finished.

As one area of work in the Church finishes for us, so another begins... perhaps less physically active or less mentally exacting... yet nevertheless, just as vital for God's work to continue here on earth. We have a life-long calling... and constant new growth in Christ.

New Life – 2
(Moving Mountains)

The gardener had never been enthusiastic about garden ornaments but his mother, a keen gardener, had several gnomes and animals in her beautiful garden. When she died, he kept a few, partly as a nostalgic reminder of his childhood.

He was doing some Autumn gardening, tidying up and planting some more miniature daffodils near to the rockery. There was his mother's stone tortoise... and, to his amazement, there were some fairly long leaves from the grape hyacinth bulbs, sticking out in all directions from underneath the tortoise.

The gardener had moved the tortoise in the summer, placing it on what he thought was a bare piece of soil. It was obviously right over the top of a clump of bulbs! Two things amazed him. One was that the bulbs already had long leaf shoots, although the flowers wouldn't appear until the Spring. The other amazing thing was that the heavy stone tortoise had not prevented or even hindered the growth of the shoots.

On piercing the surface of the soil, those shoots would have met solid stone. They were not killed off or even halted. They simply bent round until they came to the end of the stone and then they turned upwards, growing green and straight all the way round the tortoise and looking a bit like a hedgehog's spines. The slender, pointed leaves were really quite fragile. There was no way that they could move the

32

stone tortoise. They certainly could not go through it... So they went round it... They were not prevented from growing.

Are we prevented from growing when faced by obstacles? Do we stop when something seemingly insurmountable is in the way? Do we give up, make excuses, say that we really cannot manage that particular task? Our human strength is indeed rather limited... but do we underestimate God's strength? Do we prefer not even to allow God to have a go? Does a particular task seem a bit too difficult, so we think we'll leave it, thank you very much?

Whatever obstacle appears to be in our way, however insurmountable it may seem, we can overcome it with God's strength. We are not meant to do things on our own. God never intended us to be worn out by our own efforts... He needs to use us as His hands, feet, lips, heart... but He does not need our strength. His strength is more than sufficient for any task. We do not stand a chance alone. We cannot move mountains.

No way could those fragile leaf shoots move that stone tortoise. In the same way, when faced by opposition, obstacles, barriers – even as we attempt to do God's work – we do not stand a chance alone.

We cannot move mountains... but God can!

"Come to me, all who labour and are heavy laden, and I will give you rest. Take my yoke upon you and learn from me...
For my yoke is easy and my burden is light."
(Matthew 11:28-30).

The Gardener

The young office worker was back at work after her lovely holiday spent mainly out-of-doors. The sun was shining... and she was sitting looking at the various things that needed doing. She was finding it hard to put her mind to any of them. She couldn't get back into the swing of things at all.

She sat thinking about her garden and what she would have liked to have been doing at that moment. She was picturing all that she had done in it during the past days... and she suddenly had a lovely mental image of God striding about her garden with a fork in His hand... walking in that purposeful way when something needs to be done... a look of strength on His face.

During the past week, the young woman's husband had replaced several large fence panels, which had been blown down in the winds a few weeks before. It had been a big job... exposing quite a stretch of border that had been fairly neglected for a while. That had given her a whole new project... to dig up the plants, split and sort them and dig out unwanted plants, which had secretly set themselves in the border.

There had been some fairly well established plants hidden away. These had been self-set and had crowded the border. They had taken a lot of digging out. The trouble with those plants had been that they had not been noticed until they had become fairly well established, for they had grown up between the other plants. There had been the usual inevitable weeds. The soil had been heavy and flat... in need of turning over, lifting and feeding. The border had been in need of a complete overhaul to let in the light and air and to allow the plants which should be there to spread and grow to their true beauty and potential.

God is a gardener... in us... in our lives. If we allow Him to work in us... if we remain open to what He has to do... He will 'turn over' the soil of our lives so that we remain open and fresh to His Light and to the air of the Holy Spirit. It's a constant job, which can only be undertaken with our agreement. If we prefer not to allow God to touch us, we soon become overgrown and crowded inside with things that are not good for us. It does not take long for us to acquire a lot of superfluous 'growth' and, left untended, we soon become choked with things that prevent our true light shining, just as the established plants in the border were being choked and over-run by the others.

If we resist God's gardening, the sorting and clearing out can be a long, hard and sometimes painful business when He eventually gains access to our lives. Some old habits, which are not of God's choosing, can be difficult to break and the withdrawal from them can be a tearful business. Some of our talents may be being used in the wrong place and for the wrong reasons and may need uprooting, splitting and resetting for the benefit of the Church and for the growth of God's Kingdom. We may be trying to spread ourselves too thinly and need a good pruning back to focus our major gifts where they can glorify God.

Even if we feel that we do allow God reasonable access to the organisation of our lives, the need for His care and for His attention to the details is constant. We need to allow Him to hoe over the soil of our spirits so that it is kept loose and retentive, so that it can soak up His life-giving water and food. We need to allow God to weed constantly, so that any unwanted and undesirable activities or influences are quickly removed before they take firm root and choke our actions in Christ. We need to allow God to remove unwanted growth as we head off in the wrong directions, using our talents unwisely or too freely, so causing poor development. We need to be prepared to allow Him to water and feed us freely, so that we grow in Him as He wishes, tall, straight and firm, with roots which are strong and established in the rich soil of His love and care.

We are the garden individually and collectively and God is the gardener. May we always welcome His Presence in our lives as He tends and cares for us, so that we grow strong in Him.

"I am the true vine and my Father is the gardener." John 15:1

On Our Guard

The young couple had just completed a year in their new house and they had shared the excitement of seeing what the garden had to offer as the year progressed.

As the Autumn approached they began to clear the front borders and they made some interesting discoveries. During the Summer, they had been aware of a buttercup plant trying to spread into the border and they had dug it up from time to time. They had also seen lots of tiny wild pansy plants which had set themselves in the centre circle of bedding plants.

The couple had gradually taken out a few bedding plants as they had died off, but then they decided to clear them completely and turn over the soil. In amongst the summer flowers were tendrils of straggling pansies, very leggy and crawling over and among the bushy bedding plants. The flowers were pretty. Given more time, the pansies could well have taken over the border, as dozens of seedlings were already shooting up from the soil. The couple's first thought was that the pansies did not take a lot of clearing as they were shallow-rooted but, nevertheless, they must have been taking a lot of goodness out of the soil.

The buttercup had also made interesting inroads. As the couple had cleared it from the border from time to time they had not taken much notice of the fact that the buttercup was changing its direction and going into the lawn. During the early Autumn clearing they discovered a large area of buttercup growth in the lawn, partly hidden by an overhanging bush. The tendrils were easily pulled out but they had covered quite an area of the grass, killing it completely. The buttercup, too, was still showing one or two pretty flowers. As the couple dug away at the plant, they talked about how much we, as Christians, need to be constantly on our guard. They had been aware of both of those flowers during the summer but they had not given them sufficient attention. Over the weeks, the plants had surreptitiously made their way amongst the lawn and flowers, stifling, over-crowding, taking the goodness and even killing.

They were weeds and really had no place in the garden. They were a danger to the plants. By their nature they were rampant, climbing over everything else and threatening healthy growth. They were attractive and were therefore inclined to mislead the gardener, who could easily overlook the threat until it was too late.

At least these plants were shallow rooted. They could easily be pulled out and obviously had no substance. Yet, even here, there was a hidden danger.

The couple thought that they had cleared the pansies quite well. They prepared to put in their spring-flowering plants and discovered fine, white root systems left behind from the pansies... Those roots would soon begin to spread and threaten the roots of the small spring plants. The buttercups, too, had left behind a network of roots, ready for re-growth.

We have to be constantly on our guard against things which threaten to choke us and affect our healthy growth in Christ. So often we do not see the danger of things until we are caught up by the tendrils, having been lulled into a false sense of security by the outward attraction of what could, in fact, be dangerous.

We can enjoy a hobby and not see that it is sapping our spiritual growth until we suddenly realise that it has taken over the time which we used to spend with God. We can be engrossed in our work and not realise that it is depriving us of the time and energy for Christian Fellowship. We can enjoy someone's company, find their personality attractive and be quite involved in a relationship with them before we realise that, because of their non-Christian beliefs, they are, in fact, a threat to our own spirituality.

We have to make a conscious effort to break from these things or, at least, to keep a balance, for any lingering hold can soon take root again and stifle our growth as Christians.

Time-consuming work and interests take our energy and we have no quality time left for God as we sit tired and unresponsive with our Bibles. We are meant to be in the world but we always have to remember that we are not of the world. In John, chapter 17, we read Jesus' words as He prayed for His disciples. The passage begins at verse 6, but in verses 15 and 16 Jesus says,

"My prayer is not that you take them out of the world but that you protect them from the evil one. They are not of the world, even as I am not of it".

Of course we need to put our full efforts into our work. Of course we may work with people of different beliefs. Of course we are meant to socialise with non-Christians, otherwise, how can we show God to the world? It is certain that we cannot and must not attempt to retreat from this world. Jesus Himself instructed us to, "Go into all the world and preach the good news to all creation." (Mark 16:15). It is healthy to enjoy a hobby outside Church activities, for it gives us a wider perspective on life. We just need to be careful... to keep our eyes on God... to know what our priorities are... to keep them balanced... to feed daily on God's word and on Christian fellowship... to know that we are rooted firmly in Christ.

In that way there is no threat as we seek to spread God's word into the world... with one foot on the earth and one in Heaven.

Ḧearing Ḧis Voice

It felt good in the garden early on that first day of the holiday. The air was fresh and the day bright and there was nothing pressing to think about.

The usually quiet garden was not quite so peaceful because a rather large family of starlings was having its breakfast. The gardener stopped to watch... and he learnt a lot about the vocabulary of starlings. The baby birds were similar in size to their parents... and obviously very hungry. Mum and Dad were flying somewhat frantically backwards and forwards trying to satisfy their offsprings' appetites.

The babies had settled in next door's cherry tree, which overhung into the garden. Their wings were fluttering as they bounced around together amongst the branches. Suddenly, there was the rather raucous call of the parent starlings as they flew away to find food... and the young birds picked up the call.

When the parent birds returned, their beaks filled with grubs for the babies, the sound became quite deafening as the youngsters called out to the adults.

This noise and activity continued for a short time... until the cat appeared in the garden. A short, shrill sound came from the cherry tree and everything was immediately silent. It was an unusual sound for a starling to make, but it was very effective. Hungry and excited as the babies were, they immediately became still and silent at the warning call of their parents.

The cat strolled past their tree and went further down the garden. The normal call of the starlings was heard, the "all-clear", and the babies bounced around again, chattering to one another. The cat saw the parent birds returning to the tree with food and went over towards them. This time, at another command, the babies flew with one accord across the garden into the ash tree. They sat close together, still and quiet, listening for the next instruction.

It was fascinating. The starlings had such a varied vocabulary! There were a few other sounds around at the time. A cuckoo could be heard in the distance, a robin and blue tit were calling from time to time as they, too, fed their babies, a car started up... and yet those baby starlings seemed to have ears only for their parents, listening carefully for their calls... obeying each sound... even controlling their feelings of hunger and excitement if ordered to do so. They were allowed free reign if all was well... but, if necessary, they were instructed to be silent and still for their own safety... and their response was immediate. They were not distracted by any extraneous sounds. They knew what they were listening for and no other sound took their attention, nor did they take a long time to respond... considering whether to do so or not. There was no question about it!

The birds' response was amazing! Do we hear God's voice like that? We speak of listening to God's voice but do we always listen as carefully as we might... do we hear it as clearly as we should... do we obey it readily and carefully? There are different ways in which we do not hear it quite as perfectly as we would like to think we do. There are different reasons for a delayed reaction between hearing and responding.

We can seek God's guidance over a problem. We listen attentively for His response, trying to seek His answer... but we do not necessarily follow it when it comes. Do we obey without question, even if His reply is not quite what we had expected or hoped for? Do we hear God's voice and then make our own decision anyway? Do we choose the direction that is easier... more attractive... more lucrative... the obvious answer, really without God in the equation?

Perhaps it may be that we hear God's instructions quite clearly. We may be very aware that He is trying to guide us along a particular path... that He wants us to do a particular job for Him. We hear His voice. We realise that He is right... that we have no choice... even that it is certainly the best thing for us to do. Yet we hesitate before obeying. It can take a long time before we actually make a move to follow Him. There is a delayed reaction before we obey Him.

Why is that? We know that God knows best... that He always chooses the right direction for us... that He will not send us anywhere that will harm us.

Let's resolve to listen out carefully at all times for God's voice. Let's be sure to recognise it above all the other sounds around... remembering that His voice is so often the still, small voice amidst all the loud noises. Having heard His voice, let us respond immediately, instead of after dithering and weighing everything up for ages...

We know His peace only when we have listened, responded and acted in accordance to His words.

Let's do it immediately... and enjoy the permanence of His peace.

Be Noticed

Cotoneaster plants seem to attract bees.

On sunny days, the sound of the bees on the still air attracts our attention. The plants, are often alive with small bees and this hive of activity can be in complete contrast to the rest of the garden, as it sleeps in the heat of the sun.

Various things stand out as we watch:

- ❖ The perseverance and application of the bees as they fly backwards and forwards collecting pollen.
- ❖ The way in which they all know what they have to do.
- ❖ The way in which they work separately yet together, all intent on the same ultimate aim.
- ❖ The complete contrast which this very small area makes to the rest of the garden. There could be the soft sound of a wood pigeon, a butterfly stretching lazy wings to the sun, a cat lying in the shade with the cool soil on his tummy, no movement. The whole garden appears to be sleeping... except for this little section.

Shouldn't we be like that? That does not mean to say that we should never rest... but picture your Church. When others in the community have switched off from, or ignored, the full life which Christ offers... when they are all, metaphorically speaking, asleep... shouldn't we be amongst them, tirelessly working for God?

- ❖ If we persevere, even if at times we feel that we are seeing no results.
- ❖ If we support and encourage one another as we bring our separate gifts and strengths to use towards the same ultimate aim.
- ❖ If we are all individually aware of where our strengths lie and of what our contribution is and work accordingly, knowing the value of our own contribution towards the spreading of the Kingdom of God.
- ❖ Then, like the bees, we, too, shall attract attention because we shall be in stark contrast to the life going on around us. Then, we shall be seen to be a hive of activity, doing God's work.

Then, people will stop and consider, for by our actions and words we shall be noticed because we reflect God's light.

"All that is mine is thine, and what is thine is mine; and through them has my glory shone".   John 17:10, New English Bible

J am the Vine

Øne of the Minister's favourite passages in the Bible was John 15:1-8, when Jesus said, "I am the true Vine and my Father is the gardener... I am the vine; you are the branches. If a man remains in me and I in him, he will bear much fruit; apart from me you can do nothing."

The Minister had a vine in his greenhouse. In fact, during the Summer, it virtually took over half of the greenhouse. It fascinated him. In the late Autumn, he cut the vine ruthlessly back to its main stem and during the winter it stood stark and bare, with its thick, strong central stem.

Slowly, as Spring approached, green shoots began to appear and, from that point onwards, new growth was rapid and profuse. The more the vine had been cut back, the more lush was its growth. The new leaves opened, bright green and healthy, and then the fruit began to form. As the leaves opened, any remaining damaged branches began to show up because they hung limp and useless and still bare, whilst all around them the healthy shoots were flourishing. The dead branch had to be cut off because it would impede the growth of the healthy fruit. The branches which were firmly attached to the main stem thrived and produced more growth because nothing was preventing them from drawing nourishment and strength from the main stem. They were supported and fed and the transformation was wonderful.

Jesus tells us directly that we are like that. God is the gardener. Jesus is the Vine. We are all branches of that Vine, blessedly attached to Him, for we are powerless on our own. God cuts out the dead branches, the useless bits which impede our spiritual growth and He prunes the other branches hard back, so that they will flourish. If we respond positively to that pruning, we find that our new growth in Christ produces His fruit in our lives as we remain nourished and supported by Him.

Haven't we all experienced pain?... physical, mental, emotional or spiritual pain, when the hurt goes deep? These are the times which God uses for His pruning, cutting right back to free us from the superfluous growth and rubbish which make us weak and ineffective. For the Christian, suffering can produce a tremendous strength and a step towards wholeness which produces abundant fruit as we receive God's spiritual gifts.

If we remain in Christ we shall do far more abundantly than we can ever imagine. We shall bear much fruit for Him.

If we become detached, we shall be totally ineffective.

Pruning

Suddenly, there were signs of Autumn all around. The house martins were gathering on the wires – not ready to leave yet, but obviously beginning to sense something inside. There was a chill in the air in the mornings and evenings, the days were becoming noticeably shorter and the bedding plants were dying.

There is something quite satisfying about Autumn gardening. At least once the job is done, the garden remains tidy for a few months, rather than being overgrown again within days. The gardener was thinking about that as he cut back some leggy herbaceous border plants.

In the Spring, those plants had been neat, round cushions of new green leaves. As the leaves opened, so the plant itself had also grown in height and width, sending new shoots off in all directions and producing beautiful flowers on long, delicate stems. The flowers had now died, the thin flower stems had drooped to the ground and the plant had lost its shape. It had, however, grown considerably bigger in the past months and given much pleasure.

As the gardener cut off the flower stems and pruned the plant back into shape... a larger, healthy plant now, but having been in need of the removal of those straggling shoots... he thought of Christian people on their journey through life.

We begin like those compact plants... As we learn and grow, we sometimes become a bit straggly and uneven, developing more in some areas than others, making giant strides in parts of our Christian learning but not moving in others. At certain times, we produce beautiful flowers, showing our own inner radiance and God's glory. At other times, we rest in Him, receive nourishment and gain renewed inner strength. Past

46

hurts emerge and hinder our true sturdy growth. Every so often, that uneven growth has to be pruned back so that we can be healthy and complete and so that we are rounded and focused.

We are pruned back, not to where we were originally, but to a new place, further on than we were before. The pruning can be painful and hard but God prunes in love and for our own benefit, as well as for that of His Kingdom here on earth. Pruning is essential for our future health and growth as God's children. After the pruning, which can take quite a while, we are allowed to rest. We can absorb, draw breath, wait a while before we begin to grow again. Ideally, we rest in God – basking in His love and peace – not struggling to grow again – not questioning Him – but simply resting. As it says in Psalms 37:7

"Rest in the Lord and wait patiently for Him."

We tend to feel that we should be constantly moving on, striving in our own strength – but God wants us to rest sometimes and simply absorb what He has been doing in us and for us. He wants us to soak in His Word and to receive the love of fellow Christians. He will make it abundantly clear when we are to move forwards again into new growth. We shall not be able to ignore the proddings, the restlessness and the searching.

The wonderful thing about all of this is that we all move and grow and are pruned at different times. That is where we tend to differ from the plants in the garden. When we just start our Christian walk, we tend to think that we should be moving on all of the time. We tend to think that there is something wrong with us if nothing seems to "be happening" in us spiritually. In our early days, we look at other Christians who all seem to be taking leaps and bounds and we wonder what is wrong with us.

It is not always as it appears. We under-estimate God's wisdom. He knows that it is far better for us to grow at different times from one another, for the pruning to be overlapping, or even separate... some growing, others resting in God, some strong in Him, others experiencing pain of pruning... For then we can draw alongside one another, helping, explaining, supporting, listening...

We have the privilege of being part of God's garden.... and He has a very special garden.

Unconditional Love

When the lady first moved to her new house, she was thrilled when she first saw a squirrel in the garden. They were lovely to look at and most entertaining to watch. Their jerky movements and alert faces were fascinating and their antics made her smile.

However, she was not quite so thrilled as, over the months, that one visitor brought his friends and they made her garden their home. They seemed to enjoy digging up the bulbs in the Autumn, running around with those over-large 'nuts' as they stored their winter food. As Spring progressed, they enjoyed the flowers as they stripped the tulip heads from their stems. They then took up residence in the sycamore tree and methodically stripped the bark from the trees as the new sweet sap rose.

It seemed strange that they were damaging... and even running the risk of killing... that tree. It was in a lovely sunny spot. It was safe and quiet and the squirrels had made it quite cosy. They could run up and down at will, balance along the fence and dig in the garden. There was more than enough food for them amongst the plants and bulbs with tender young shoots growing. They had a comfortable existence, so why were they destroying it? Why were they harming something which was helping them, something which was supporting them?

Why do we hurt those whom we love? There is an old song which says "we always hurt the one we love." For a fleeting moment it seems rather strange, something of a paradox, but then we realise that it isn't really. It's when we feel safe with people, when we know them really well, that we tend to hurt them.

There seem to be several different reasons why we hurt the people who are closest to us. We all know the sudden outburst of anger expressed when someone we care about appears after an unexpected delay. We have been waiting for them... felt concern as the anticipated time of arrival goes by. We begin to wonder what might have arisen, picture various possible reasons why the person could be late without explanation... We feel concern, love... yet, as soon as they walk into the house, our anxiety is expressed in a raised voice and a reprimand. We give the totally opposite impression from the one which we intended. The person who is late and probably under pressure because of the situation, feels hurt and upset by the greeting, when all they wanted was a relaxed and caring welcome! Ill feeling can arise! It is because we care that we do these things.

Another reason why we hurt those whom we love is because we feel safe with them. We can let go because we know we are secure, accepted and loved for who we are. There is a great deal of love between people when they can really show their feelings, express their hurts, say what is uppermost in their hearts... in the knowledge that it will be received and understood in love... without ridicule, anger or a lessening of feelings.

We are all in some situations where we have to keep a control of our feelings. We cannot always express ourselves truly and fully wherever we are. It is often essential that we keep a certain amount of self-control and display a social acceptability in our dealings with others. So, unfortunately, it can be our closest, loved people who receive the flak after a bad experience at work or if we are tired. We need the release and they understand. Sometimes, though, this release doesn't simply come in an outpouring of what has gone wrong. It can come in unfair irritability or loss of temper with them over something trivial... out of all the pent-up frustrations of the day. We can hear ourselves 'going on' too much... but we can't stop. We hurt our loved ones... and we hurt God by our behaviour... Yet they still love us... as He does...

We feel an overwhelming, genuine sorrow after such events. We seek forgiveness and we see God's wonderful strength in people as they forgive unconditionally. They still love and accept us and the relationship can, in fact, be enhanced... as we grow to know one another more deeply... as we share all the facets of our humanity.

That is not to belittle the pain when our loved ones hurt us. It is painful. We do struggle with the hurt... and it can take a little while to recover! Yet it is, in fact, a privilege... a God-given privilege... to be on the receiving end of someone's so-called negative feelings... their anger, loss of patience, frustration, irritability, abrasiveness. It means that they feel loved, secure and accepted.

It shows a picture of God's love too for His love is unconditional, as well.

Bloom where you are Planted

From time to time, many of us may feel the desire to move house. Some of us get itchy feet and have the odd yen to live in a completely different place. The elderly man was thinking about that when he was in his garden. He stood looking at his laburnum tree. It was self-set and had gone undetected amongst the poplar trees for a number of years. The trunk and branches were spindly and, as a sapling, it had not produced any flowers. Suddenly, about four years ago, the yellow blooms had shown up at the end of the garden and the man had gone out to investigate. He had found a very attractive tree, which he had neither planted nor tended. It became a constant source of pleasure mixed with the amazement that it survived in a rather difficult position, with large poplar trees overshadowing it.

"Bloom where you are planted"... Those words had become very meaningful to the man. God puts us in a particular place for a specific reason. Even if we do not see it at the time, we are placed where He wants and needs us to be. We may sometimes be in a certain place and have a particular plan in mind, only to find ourselves moving, or changing direction. We may wonder why. We may even feel that it is not what we wished or had in mind... yet it is in God's hands.

The man sometimes wondered why he had spent a period of time in a particular place, because it had not really been through choice. It was easy, though, for him to remember that it had been a time much used by God for his own spiritual growth and understanding and a time of drawing closer to Him for support.

The man knew that that time had been used. Not only for him, then. Not only for any way in which, through God's grace, he had been able to help others, then... but for the way in which he had grown in God from that experience in order to spread His Kingdom later. God uses every situation... every opportunity... every experience that we have... and He asks us to 'bloom' where we are at the time.

We are not meant to sit back or hide. We have a mission... and that is to work for God's Kingdom... to show Him to the world. Yes, we do need to be able to sit back and receive at times... to be fed... rested... nurtured. That is partly for our own spiritual growth, partly so that we can absorb God's love and learn more about Him... but it is also very much so that we can take God out into the world and show His love to others.

We all have so many gifts. They are not all necessarily what we would call 'world-changing' gifts... but it is absolutely vital that we use them in our daily lives, for they do change the world. 'From whom much is given, much is expected'... and God has given us so much. We only have to pause for a moment and reflect individually on the many blessings which He pours on us each day to realise just how much He has given to us... and so, for Him, we bloom where we are planted... growing in the fertile soil of His love and care... nourished by His eternal supply of Living Water... supported by the strength of His arms. We can then reach out and be instrumental in the growth of His Kingdom in whatever capacity He desires.

Our gifts may include such things as a friendly smile, the right word or a good cup of tea. They may involve such things as preaching, listening or advising. All our gifts are the same size in God's eyes, equally essential and valuable. All play a vital part in His plan. He wants and requires everyone to be involved in His work... now... here... where we are planted. "The time is now and we are here."

It is so exciting to see one another grow in Christ. As we make our spiritual journey together, we guide, support and advise one another... and we have the delight of seeing the transformation. Of course, we remain the same in many ways... the basic person, originally met, known and loved... but we see the sharp edges smoothed and rounded as God refines us.

"Make me like a precious stone,
crystal clear and finely honed,
Life of Jesus shining through,
Giving glory back to you.
Mission Praise 382

We see the natural gifts developed and transformed into spiritual ones. We see the healing as we move towards wholeness and we see the personal growth as we gain in confidence in God... as we depend more and more on Him, stepping out in faith in whatever we are asked to do.

God puts us where He wants us to be. He feeds and waters us with fellowship, shared worship, mutual love, care and support, spiritual blessings and His constant flow of Living Water. It is for the advantage

and delight of one another that we should bloom where we are planted...
and it is for the furtherance of God's Kingdom and for His great joy and
glory.

Transformation

The Minister stood alone in the church. It was quiet, peaceful and so very beautiful. It was the Friday night of the weekend of the Flower Festival. The flower arrangers had used their gifts to create such lovely displays. The whole church was filled with flowers... glorifying God.

The church was a beautiful building. He thought how blessed they were with reminders of people's God-given talents whenever they stood in the church. There were the colourful windows, the skilful stonework and carpentry, the wonder of workmanship in different materials and for different purposes. Yet, on that special Friday night even the beauty of that building was transformed.

The peace of the Lord hung over everything as the colour and scent of flowers permeated the building. There was not a corner untouched... and the reflection of God's light in the whites and yellows of so many flowers lit up the church. There was the peaceful stillness of the blue and the warmth of pink... and masses of green.

God's perfection seen in each leaf and flower. The visual interpretation of verses from the Bible pleased the eye and warmed the soul... lamps, oil, sandals, musical instruments, fish and other living creatures. The Church was transformed as the very fibre of that building praised God...

... Just as we are transformed when we praise God...

... Just as we are transformed when Jesus enters our lives.

The verse from Psalm 107:35 –

"He turned the desert into pools of water and the parched ground into flowing springs",

provided a visual interpretation of that transformation for all to see.

The brown, barren area of the arrangement showed no life at all. It was bleak, empty and dry... but when water flowed into such an area, a miraculous transformation took place... new life blossomed, straight and lush. So it is with us. Without Christ in our lives we, too, are dry and empty but once the word of God enters our lives and dwells richly within us, it transforms our dryness into a beautiful oasis where sweet water flows freely and where beautiful growth flourishes.

We become alive when we were previously dead. We become fertile instead of infertile. We take on a new life and beauty in Christ.

"O Lord, your loveliness,
Changing all my ugliness,
O Lord, I receive your love."

The potential is always there. The spark of God is there, inside each one of us, ready to be fanned into a flame. We have the potential to be beautiful in Him... to be creative. We go about our daily lives using the gifts which God has given us, whether we acknowledge them as His gifts or not. We do create. We can build relationships. We do live our daily lives... but there is an empty hole... an unfulfilled area... something unfinished and unresponsive. We simply need the touch of our Lord to transform our lives... the caress of His tenderness to change our ugliness into loveliness... the gentle waft of the Holy Spirit to turn the spark into a blaze...

And suddenly, we live for Him. When that inner hole is filled by the Holy Spirit, everything falls into place. We no longer have ourselves at the centre of our lives, but God. We no longer do things for ourselves, but for God. We no longer do things in our own strength, but in God's.

"I have been crucified with Christ: the life I now live is not my life, but the life which Christ lives in me; and my present bodily life is lived by faith in the Son of God, who loved me and gave Himself for me." Galatians 2:19-20.

We no longer desire anything for ourselves, but for God... and that is a life transformed. The whole emphasis is changed. Placed in God's hands, a life changes. We may still do the same work, but we do it with a different spirit and vision. In essence, we may still have the same routine, but the emphasis on the use of our time becomes different. Our relationships may remain superficially the same... but we are different and our attitude towards people changes. We look at them with God's eyes. We try to behave towards them as Christ would, for He lives in us...

He has transformed us... and the world cannot help but see!

Thank You

There had been a spell of hot, sticky weather. Everyone and everything was beginning to wilt. Part of the lawn had turned brown under the ash tree and, although the tubs had been watered, they were looking decidedly dry.

So it was something of a relief all round, when the gardener woke up to heavy rain. It seemed strange, although it really hadn't been so long since there had been a lot of rain. Everyone had quickly become accustomed to seeing a blue sky and bright sunshine. The gardener stood at the back door watching the rain... smelling the lovely freshness of the rain on the ground... seeing the garden suddenly become a hive of activity.

He was amazed. It was so busy. It actually looked a bit like nature's rush hour! The garden became full of birds... the trees shook with their movement as they landed and took off. The two bird baths were occupied by birds drinking thirstily and attending to their ablutions. The lawn was full of birds scurrying about, heads on one side, bright eyes alert, listening for worms, pulling them up and scratching around for different grubs. It was fascinating...

There were other signs of renewed vigour, as dragonflies flew around and bees droned amongst the flowers. The plants were also beginning to be refreshed by this downpour, drinking in the welcome water, lifting their heads and losing their dusty appearance. There was so much activity as the garden said "thank you" for the rain.

The gardener thought of the desert and its transformation when it is watered. Those dry, arid areas of land change so quickly as water falls. Flowers literally open as one watches and wildlife appears at pools of water to bathe and drink. He thought of the beauty of such a scene as the desert springs to life... and he thought of our similar transformation when Jesus pours His life-giving water into and over us. How beautiful we become as we blossom and flourish in Him.

There are so many references in the Old Testament to the desert and to God's promise to water it so that it brings forth life. The life of the desert is so particularly beautiful and amazing because it is in such stark contrast to what was there before the rain came. So with us. No matter what our lives were like before God touched them, they were in stark contrast to the glory of our lives after we know Him.

The gardener also thought... Do we say "Thank you"?

As he stood at the door, looking at the garden in the rain, everything out there seemed to be saying, "thank you". As the ground thirstily drank in the water and as the birds hurried around, there was a tangible sense of joy and thanksgiving. Do we always remember to thank our God for His gifts... or do we sometimes take them for granted? Do we always thank Him for answered prayer... or are we sometimes in a hurry and forget?

Our day should, in a way, be one long act of thankfulness for all that God gives to us. We know that all that we have and see comes from Him. From the moment we open our eyes, we are blessed by the gift of life, of a new day with all its promise, of our family, food and clothes. We could obviously go on, for the list is endless and the way in which we use and fill that day is, in itself, an act of thanksgiving as we honour God's generosity by using it to His glory.

Yet it is good to say, "thank you", too... for the everyday things, for the not-so-everyday things, and for answered prayer. Our day can be a constant asking... as we send up brief requests to God... arrow prayers for guidance, support, wisdom, a parking space, comfort for someone. Do the swift "thank you's" go up just as quickly as we hurry on to the next event of the day? Are we as quick to acknowledge the many swift answers to our requests?

Then there are the "bigger" things... specific prayer about matters which concern us... the problems of our family and friends, the health of those we love, situations at work... cares too numerous to mention. We hand them all to God, sometimes in such an out-pouring of concern, love and desire. We see such graciousness as God responds to us with peace, compassion and wisdom... And do we say "thank you"?

Yes, we often do...

The gardener had been talking with a friend. He had mentioned that he had been thanking God for answered prayer... even when God had answered in a way that was not what he had in mind! God had so obviously presented an opportunity, an answer to prayer, that was so much the opposite of what the friend had had in mind, that the answer was momentarily almost missed because of its 'disguise'!

God answers our prayers. We know that. He listens to us. He knows what is best.

He loves to hear us ask... He loves to please us...

He also loves to hear us say "thank you"...

Let's try not to forget.

So many of the New Testament writers urge us in all things to give thanks to our God. In 1 Thessalonians, chapter 5, we read those lovely words:

"Be joyful always; pray continually; give thanks in all circumstances, for this is God's will for you in Christ Jesus." (verses 16-18)

Joy

It's only a little word... "joy"... yet it holds such a depth of meaning. The lady was gardening when she felt that sudden surge of joy pass through her... and so many thoughts went through her mind.

The cause of her joy that day was the sight of a poppy just beginning to open. Her friend had given her some poppy seeds from the garden some time ago... They were special poppies and the lady so wanted them to grow. She was a bit doubtful because her garden was not a very good one in which to scatter seeds... The soil was heavy and she tended to clear little shoots when she weeded. The poppies in her friends' garden were doing well... but she couldn't really remember where hers were... and she didn't like to say anything!

The lady walked into her garden. The weather was glorious... warm and sunny. This was her first opportunity to garden properly for nearly two weeks and it was good to feel her body relax in the warmth instead of shivering in the cold weather and endless rain of late. She walked round the garden, savouring the flowers and there, straight and beautiful, was the pink poppy... The colour was just beginning to show through the cracks of the sepals.

The lady felt a surge of joy... It was a mixture of feelings... relief that at least one of the poppies had survived... pleasure in the new plant... delight in the truly beautiful leaves and show of colour. She crouched down to savour the perfection of it and she felt joy. She thought of C.S. Lewis' book, "Surprised by Joy"...

That is precisely what joy does... It surprises. That is why it's just that special bit different from feelings like "pleasure" and "happiness". It's more than that. The dictionary definition gives "extreme gladness" as a description of joy... and that is exactly what one feels... <u>extreme</u> gladness.

When we experience such feelings, we want to rejoice... We feel so good, so excited, so thrilled that we want to make a noise about it. We want to share our news and our pleasure with others. It's too wonderful to keep to ourselves. We don't want to carry on quietly as before, as though nothing had happened... The lady went off to tell people about her poppy!

She thought of the times in our lives when we feel joy... the birth of a baby... an engagement between a man and a woman... a personal achievement... a glorious view... a special friendship... We want to tell people. We want to share our experiences... our feelings. We want them to know of our "extreme gladness."

She thought of us and God... for joy is the word so often used about our relationship with Him. Jesus told various stories to describe God's joy in us. He spoke of the woman searching for her silver coin and of the lengths to which she went in order to find it. She swept the house until she discovered her coin and when she had done so, she called to everyone around.

"Rejoice with me, I have found my lost coin".

Jesus adds, "In the same way, I tell you, there is rejoicing in the presence of the angels of God over one sinner who repents."
Luke 15:8-10

There is the famous story of the lost sheep, in which the shepherd leaves his flock to search for the one sheep that is missing. His joy when he finds the sheep is unmistakable and contagious. In Luke chapter 15, we read,

"And when he finds it, he joyfully puts it on his shoulders and goes home. Then he calls his friends and neighbours together and says, "Rejoice with me; I have found my lost sheep", verses 5 and 6.

Again, Jesus comments that
"There will be more rejoicing in heaven over one sinner who repents than over ninety-nine righteous people who do not need to repent." Verse 7.

The story of the Prodigal Son in Luke 15:11-32, illustrates so totally God's utter joy over each of His children. Whenever we turn to Him, his heart is filled with that extreme gladness and the angels in heaven rejoice... over us... each one of us! God delights in our presence. His heart is filled with joy...

We, too, can feel joy at being with Him. This is expressed in those lovely lines of "To be in Your Presence":
"To rest in Your presence,
Not rushing away.

To cherish each moment,
Here I would stay." Spring Harvest 1993, no. 128

The very sound of those soft words speaks of joy in the company of God. "To cherish", means "to hold dear" and what a wonderful thought it is that we can hold dear every moment that we spend in God's presence... that we can find joy in His company.

It is truly breath-taking... that the God who created heaven and earth can experience such joy when each of His children repents and turns to Him. His joy is so great that He wants to share it and all the angels in heaven join with Him to celebrate. He experiences joy whenever we come to Him in prayer... whenever we look to Him, ask His advice...

Our God knows joy when He is in our presence. What a humbling thought! We, too, feel that same joy... joy in the knowledge that we are safe in His care... joy in the fact that we can draw close to God and learn from Him... joy in the assurance that He loves us... Joy in His very company.

... And when we experience joy, we want to share it... with one another and with the world.

"I will go Lord, if you lead me;
I will hold your people in my heart".

Shine, Jesus, Shine

The man mowing the lawn found his attention caught by a butterfly landing on a bush. He watched as it moved around amongst the yellow flowers until it found a favourable spot to settle.

The butterfly twisted and turned and then suddenly opened the full splendour of its beautiful wings to the sun and remained quite still. It was at such an angle that the full warmth and light of the sun beamed down on the largest possible area of the butterfly's body. It lay motionless for a long time, soaking up the warmth.

The man considered the way in which the butterfly had adjusted its position for maximum benefit as it naturally extended itself to absorb the sun's heat and light. He looked round the garden with the sudden realisation that everything naturally turns to face that wonderful source of life for all living things. Every flower in the garden had its face directed towards the sun... so many flower heads... yellow, orange, pink, purple, blue... all turned upwards, facing the light.

It is a simple rule of nature, of course. In order to grow and flourish, every living thing needs light and warmth. The man thought of the primary school experiments, when he had grown seedlings and put them into different situations to see how their growth was affected. Some plants were put in a cold, dark place and they did not thrive very well at all... and eventually, they died.

That's like us and God. As Christians, we need the warmth and light which exudes from God. We need to be able to bask in Him as the butterfly basked in the sun. We need to open ourselves up so that we can absorb our God into our very beings. As Christians, we need to lift up our heads and seek God's face. Human beings tend to walk around with their heads down, looking at the ground just a few paces in front of their feet. We must learn to lift up our heads and turn our faces to God's warmth and light, so that it can shine upon us. In this way, His light and warmth will nourish us and help us to grow in His love and will. When our faces are turned to God, they can also reflect His light to the world and attract other people to Him.

If our faces are turned away from God, we fail to feel His light and warmth. We are therefore deprived of some of our basic needs from

Him and we do not flourish and thrive as His children. We do not grow as Christians... and the world does not see God in us.

Let us at all times lift up our heads and, like the butterfly, present the biggest possible area to our source of light and warmth. Let us seek God's face and allow His light to radiate from us. Not only shall we flourish in His light and warmth, but the world, too, will see something special. People will see our God reflected in us... What a wonderful thought.

What a privilege.

"This day I call heaven and earth as witnesses against you that I have set before you life and death, blessings and curses. Now choose life, so that you and your children may live and that you may love the Lord your God, listen to His voice and hold fast to Him. For the Lord is your life..." Deuteronomy 30:15-20.

MOORLEY'S

We are growing publishers, adding several new titles to our list each year. We also undertake private publications and commissioned works.

Our range of publications includes:

Books of Verse:
Devotional Poetry
Recitations

Drama
Bible Plays
Sketches
Nativity Plays
Passiontide Plays
Easter Plays
Demonstrations

Resource Books
Assembly Material
Songs and Musicals
Children's Addresses
Prayers and Graces
Daily Readings
Books for Speakers

Activity Books
Quizzes
Puzzles
Painting Books

Church Stationery
Notice Books
Cradle Rolls
Hymn Board Numbers

Please send a stamped addressed envelope (approx. 9" x 6") for the current catalogue or consult your local Christian Bookshop who should stock or be able to order our titles.